Journaling My Prayers

Journaling My Prayers

Published by Gatekeeper Press
2167 Stringtown Rd, Suite 109
Columbus, OH 43123-2989
www.GatekeeperPress.com

The interior formatting, typesetting, and editorial work for this book are entirely the product of the author. Gatekeeper Press did not participate in and is not responsible for any aspect of these elements.

ISBN: 9781662901492

Therefore I tell you, whatever you ask for in prayer, believe that you have received it, and it will be yours.
Mark 11:24

As you write down and journal your fervent prayers, see it as a way of communicating with God. I pray you will receive the answers you're seeking.

Temiika D. Gipson

_____

_____

_____

_____

_____

_____

_____

_____

_____

_____

_____

_____

_____

Rejoice always, pray continually, give thanks in all circumstances...1 Thessalonians 5:16-18

_____

_____

_____

_____

_____

_____

_____

_____

_____

_____

_____

_____

_____

Do not be anxious about anything, but in every situation, by prayer and petition, with thanksgiving, present your requests to God. Philippians 4:6

_____

_____

_____

_____

_____

_____

_____

_____

_____

_____

_____

_____

_____

Devote yourselves to prayer, being watchful and
thankful. Colossians 4:2

_____

_____

_____

_____

_____

_____

_____

_____

_____

_____

_____

_____

Be joyful in hope, patient in affliction, faithful in prayer. Romans 12:12

_____

_____

_____

_____

_____

_____

_____

_____

_____

_____

_____

_____

This is the confidence we have in approaching God:
that if we ask anything according to his will, he
hears us. 1 John 5:14

_____

_____

_____

_____

_____

_____

_____

_____

_____

_____

_____

_____

_____

_____

Call to me and I will answer you and tell you great
and unsearchable things you do not know.
Jeremiah 33:3

_____

_____

_____

_____

_____

_____

_____

_____

_____

_____

_____

_____

_____

_____

And if we know that he hears us—whatever we
ask—we know that we have what we asked of him.
1 John 5:15

_____

_____

_____

_____

_____

_____

_____

_____

_____

_____

_____

_____

_____

_____

_____

The LORD is near to all who call on him, to all who call on him in truth. Psalm 145:18

_____

_____

_____

_____

_____

_____

_____

_____

_____

_____

_____

_____

_____

_____

_____

_____

Therefore I tell you, whatever you ask for in prayer,
believe that you have received it, and it will be yours.
Mark 11:24

_____

_____

_____

_____

_____

_____

_____

_____

_____

_____

_____

_____

_____

_____

_____

But when you ask, you must believe and not doubt, because the one who doubts is like a wave of the sea, blown and tossed by the wind. James 1:6

_____

_____

_____

_____

_____

_____

_____

_____

_____

_____

_____

_____

_____

_____

I cried out to him with my mouth; his praise was on my tongue. Psalm 66:17

When hard pressed, I cried to the Lord; he brought
me into a spacious place. Psalm 118:5

_____

_____

_____

_____

_____

_____

_____

_____

_____

_____

_____

_____

_____

_____

Lord, hear my prayer, listen to my cry for mercy;
in your faithfulness and righteousness come to my
relief. Psalm 143:1

_____

_____

_____

_____

_____

_____

_____

_____

_____

_____

_____

_____

_____

_____

_____

But this kind does not go out except by prayer and fasting. Matthew 17:21

And I will do whatever you ask in my name, so that the Father may be glorified in the Son. John 14:13

_____

_____

_____

_____

_____

_____

_____

_____

_____

_____

_____

_____

_____

Watch and pray so that you will not fall into
temptation. The spirit is willing, but the flesh is weak.
Matthew 26:41

_____

_____

_____

_____

_____

_____

_____

_____

_____

_____

_____

_____

_____

In the morning, LORD, you hear my voice; in the morning I lay my requests before you and wait expectantly. Psalm 5:3

_____

_____

_____

_____

_____

_____

_____

_____

_____

_____

_____

_____

_____

_____

So we fasted and petitioned our God about this,
and he answered our prayer. Ezra 8:23

_____

_____

_____

_____

_____

_____

_____

_____

_____

_____

_____

_____

_____

"I am the Lord's servant," Mary answered. "May your word to me be fulfilled." Then the angel left her. Luke 1:38

_____

_____

_____

_____

_____

_____

_____

_____

_____

_____

_____

_____

_____

_____

So Peter was kept in prison, but the church was earnestly praying to God for him. Acts 12:5

_____

_____

_____

_____

_____

_____

_____

_____

_____

_____

_____

_____

They devoted themselves to the apostles' teaching
and to fellowship, to the breaking of bread and to
prayer. Acts 2:42

_____

_____

_____

_____

_____

_____

_____

_____

_____

_____

_____

_____

_____

Look to the LORD and his strength; seek his face always. 1 Chronicles 16:11

_____

_____

_____

_____

_____

_____

_____

_____

_____

_____

_____

_____

_____

Keep me as the apple of Your eye; hide me in
the shadow of Your wings. Psalm 17:8

_____

_____

_____

_____

_____

_____

_____

_____

_____

_____

_____

_____

Ask and it will be given to you; seek and you will
find; knock and the door will be opened to you.
Matthew 7:7

_____

_____

_____

_____

_____

_____

_____

_____

_____

_____

_____

_____

I sought the LORD, and he answered me; he
delivered me from all my fears. Psalm 34:4

_____

_____

_____

_____

_____

_____

_____

_____

_____

_____

_____

_____

_____

Take delight in the LORD, and he will give you the desires of your heart. Psalm 37:4

_____

_____

_____

_____

_____

_____

_____

_____

_____

_____

_____

_____

_____

You will seek me and find me when you seek me
with all your heart. Jeremiah 29:13

_____

_____

_____

_____

_____

_____

_____

_____

_____

_____

_____

_____

_____

If any of you lack wisdom, you should ask God,
who gives generously to all without finding
fault, and it will be given to you. James 1:5

_____

_____

_____

_____

_____

_____

_____

_____

_____

_____

_____

_____

_____

But seek first his kingdom and his righteousness,
and all these things will be given to you as well.
Matthew 6:33

_____

_____

_____

_____

_____

_____

_____

_____

_____

_____

_____

_____

_____

If you remain in me and my words remain in you,
ask whatever you wish, and it will be done for you.
John 15:7

_____

_____

_____

_____

_____

_____

_____

_____

_____

_____

_____

_____

At Gibeon the LORD appeared to Solomon during
the night in a dream, and God said, "Ask for
whatever you want me to give you." 1 Kings 3:5

_____

_____

_____

_____

_____

_____

_____

_____

_____

_____

_____

_____

_____

I call out to the LORD, and he answers me from his
holy mountain. Psalm 3:4

_____

_____

_____

_____

_____

_____

_____

_____

_____

_____

_____

_____

Answer me when I call to you, my righteousness
God. Give me relief from my distress; have mercy
on me and hear my prayer. Psalm 4:1

The righteous cry out, and the LORD hears them;
he delivers them from all their troubles.
Psalm 34:17

_____

_____

_____

_____

_____

_____

_____

_____

_____

_____

_____

_____

Never be lacking in zeal, but keep your spiritual
fervor, serving the Lord. Romans 12:11

_____

_____

_____

_____

_____

_____

_____

_____

_____

_____

_____

_____

_____

Then you will call on me and come and pray to
me, and I will listen to you. Jeremiah 29:12

_____

_____

_____

_____

_____

_____

_____

_____

_____

_____

_____

_____

_____

You will pray to him, and he will hear you, and you will fulfill your vows. Job 22:27

_____

_____

_____

_____

_____

_____

_____

_____

_____

_____

_____

_____

I call on you, my God, for you will answer me; turn your ear to me and hear my prayer. Psalm 17:6

_____

_____

_____

_____

_____

_____

_____

_____

_____

_____

_____

_____

He will respond to the prayer of the destitute; he will
not despise their plea. Psalm 102:17

Made in the USA
Columbia, SC
19 June 2020